BELIEVING GOD FOR A HOUSE

Chad Gonzales

Scripture quotations taken from the New King James Version. Copyright © 1982 by Thomas Nelson, Inc. Used by permission. All rights reserved.

Scripture quotations taken from the Amplified® Bible, Copyright © 1954, 1958, 1962, 1964, 1965, 1987 by The Lockman Foundation. Used by permission." (www.Lockman.org)

Scripture taken from The Message. Copyright 1993, 1994, 1995, 1996, 2000, 2001, 2002. Used by permission of NavPress Publishing Group."

Scripture taken from the HOLY BIBLE, NEW INTERNATIONAL VERSION®. Copyright © 1973, 1978, 1984 Biblica. Used by permission of Zondervan. All rights reserved.

Scripture quotations are taken from the Holy Bible, New Living Translation, copyright 1996, 2004. Used by permission of Tyndale House Publishers, Inc., Wheaton, Illinois 60189. All rights reserved.

Believing God For A House
ISBN: 978-1-7354232-0-3
Copyright © 2020 by Chad W. Gonzales
Chad Gonzales Ministries
www.ChadGonzales.com

Printed in the United States of America. All rights reserved under International Copyright Law. Contents and/or cover may not be reproduced in whole or in part in any form without the express written consent of the Publisher or Author.

TABLE OF CONTENTS

Our Story   5

SECTION ONE: God's Will For Your House

Chapter One   9
The Foundation Of Your Faith

Chapter Two   11
You Need A House

Chapter Three   17
A Beautiful House

Chapter Four   33
A House Filled With Nice Things

Chapter Five   43
A Safe House

Chapter Six   45
A Big House

Chapter Seven   55
A Debt Free House

Chapter Eight   61
The Substance Of Things

SECTION TWO: Receiving Your House

Chapter Nine   71
Get Your Hopes Up

Chapter Ten   77
Stop Considering Your Circumstances

Chapter Eleven   81
Start Declaring What Is Yours

Chapter Twelve   85
Be Led By The Holy Spirit

Chapter Thirteen   91
Increase Your Giving

Chapter Fourteen   103
Start Praising God

OUR STORY

When Lacy and I married, I was twenty six years old and she was twenty years old and I was severely in debt because of college. Not only did I have debt, I had a serious poverty mindset. I had never really heard much about God's will concerning finances nor had I ever learned anything about business or real estate. I thought my only way out of poverty was education and hard work so that is what I did.

Throughout our marriage, we tried various ways in regards to obtaining the house that we wanted but things just never worked out. I had this idea that either I would work really hard and one day before we retired, we would be able to save up enough to have our dream house or just maybe we would win the lottery!

Frustrated and fed up, I began seeking God about finances. Through that journey, I began to discover some of the wonderful promises God has for us regarding our money; however, I had no idea there was so much in the Bible about houses. I began to discover that not only did God want us to have a big, beautiful house but He also wanted it filled with nice things and He wanted it paid for!

Over a period of eight years of not only meditating on these Scriptures but also being led by the Holy Spirit in our giving as well as His plan for our lives, we went from being over $150,000 in debt and losing our house to foreclosure, to having our debts paid off and owning a one million dollar home - and all of this happened while making $60,000 a year at my job! We are living proof of "If you be willing and obedient, you will eat the good of the land!"

I wish someone would have told me about some of these truths regarding God's will for our house at a young age. I remember first reading these Scriptures in my Bible and thinking, "How come no one ever told me about this?" I would have done things so much more differently when I was younger, but I am thankful I found out while my son is young enough that I can pass them on to him. I'm also thankful that I can pass these truths on to you! Let's get ready to get your house!

SECTION ONE

GOD'S WILL FOR YOUR HOUSE

CHAPTER 1
THE FOUNDATION
OF YOUR FAITH

Almost everyone falls into three categories when it comes to housing: (1) wanting to buy their first house (2) wanting to buy a bigger house (3) wanting to pay off their house. If you have been renting for a long time and you're tired of not only throwing your money away but also dealing with a landlord, I have good news for you: God wants you to have your own house! If you have a growing family and your house is too small or you just simply want a bigger, nicer home, I have good news for you: God wants you to have a bigger house! If you are like the vast majority of people who own their home but still have a mortgage, I have good news for you: God wants your house paid off!

Throughout this book, I am going to show you scripture after scripture and prove beyond a doubt that God wants you to have a beautiful, spacious, debt free house. However, in order for you to believe and release your faith for it, you need to know God's will on this particular issue.

> **1 John 5:14 NKJV**
> **Now this is the confidence that we have in Him, that if we ask anything according to His will, He hears us.**

Faith begins where the will of God is known. If you don't know what His will is on the issue, you can't have faith for it. If you want to know what God's will is, then you need to go to His Word for His Word is His will. There are a lot of people that will try and tell you what God's will is and yet it isn't in the Bible.

It doesn't matter what people have to say; you need to find out what God's Word says. For instance, some people say God wants His people broke - that God wants His people poor and humble. The other day, I was reading a newspaper article in which a prominent leader within a certain denomination said, "God wants a poor church that can support the poor people." I wondered what he was smoking when he said that!

How are you going to give financially when you don't have anything to give? You can't be poor and support the poor. You need some substance and material things to support the poor. You can't give when you don't have anything to give. Am I missing something here? God wanting me poor so I can support the poor is just plain stupid. No, if you just read your Bible, you will find that God wants you rich so you can be a blessing to other people. One of the ways you can not only become rich but also take care of a very important need is to have your very own house.

CHAPTER 2
YOU NEED A HOUSE

Philippians 4:19 AMP
And my God will liberally supply (fill until full) your every need according to His riches in glory in Christ Jesus.

God tells us He will supply all of our needs. Well, would you say that a house is a need? Certainly it is. You need a place to live right? It would be hard to find someone who would disagree with you in that a house is a need. Yet, here is where the opinions of religious people begin to show up, especially if it's a preacher buying a house. If you grew up in church like I did, you grew up around a lot of people that thought Christians were supposed to be poor. They would say, "Well, yes, God wants you to have a place to live - but you don't need anything that nice." People will agree that you need a house, but the opinions vary widely and sharply as to the dividing line between need and want.

How many times have you heard someone say, "God said He would meet all of your needs; not your wants!" So what square footage does it go from need to want? Please let me know where that is in Scripture? How big does that roof need to be in order to fit God's guidelines of my needs? After all, if it's simply about needing a roof over my head, a mobile home or apartment will do. Actually, we could go even further and just get a big tent. Of course, we don't want to be too extravagant because there are 2 and 3 room tents. Can it have multiple sleeping spaces or is that too big to fit under the category of "needs?" Or should I just get a cardboard box and use scraps of junk to make a shelter?

The problem with questions like this is that it gets into an area that God doesn't care about it. Why would God have a problem if your house was made out of brick, wood or concrete? Do you really think He cares about how many square feet your house is? Actually, Psalms 37:4 says, "Delight yourself also in the Lord, and He will give you the desires of your heart." If you want 3,000 sq feet instead of 1,500 sq ft...who cares; God certainly doesn't!

Religion Will Make You Stupid

You know, I firmly believe that some Christians are really smart until they walk into church and then they just get plain stupid. People get stupid because they put on their religious clothes and start looking at things through their religious glasses. All of a sudden, the same people who work in the medical profession trying to keep people healthy - they start telling you that healing isn't God's will. The same people going to work each day to make money - they tell you that God doesn't want you to prosper. The same people who are living way beyond their means and are one paycheck from bankruptcy - they throw a fit when you pay cash for a used car. The same people who will mock you for having too large of a house will be the same ones to gladly accept it if someone gave them the same house. Friends, religion will make you stupid.

God Is Excessive

Don't tell me that God wants me to have a house but He doesn't want it too extravagant - God is extravagant! When God gives, He gives excessively, abundantly, lavishly; He gives too much! Everything God does is way over the top.

Have you ever looked up into the sky at night and counted all the stars? There are billions and billions of stars! Look at creation and see how lavish and excessive God created things. Look how much water is on the planet. Don't listen to all the worriers in the world saying we will run out of water. God knew how much water we would need; He then gave that amount plus an excessive amount more just because that's the way He does things.

God made heaven with streets of gold and put walls around the city made of extravagant jewels. Even when you get to Heaven, I'm sure there will be people standing at the gate saying, "Well, that's just a little excessive!"

When Jesus multiplied the bread and fish, it was excessive! There were twelve baskets left over for the boy who gave his lunch to Jesus. When Jesus told Peter to cast his nets over and catch some fish, there were so many fish that Peter's boat began to sink and the net began to break! Even when we look at salvation - it was over the top! Jesus didn't come to help you a little bit; He came to radically save you and change your life.

God Is A Good Father

On top of that, God is a good Father! How prideful and just dumb can we be to want good things for our kids but then turn around and think it is God's will for us to be broke, sick and living in a shack. Again, most of the people who would say that are working hard at their job for money, going to the doctor when they get sick, and wishing they could have a bigger, nicer house.

I don't know of any parent who would wish for their child to be living in a run down house, much less having to rent a house for twenty years because they weren't in a position to buy one. If you were in a position to do so, I guarantee you that if you had kids, you would buy them a house if you could. We love our children and want to see them not only well taken care of, but we also want to see them go way beyond where we are at. If it's your will for your child, how much more so your Heavenly Father?

You Need A House

Three Reasons God Wants You To Have A House

There are a number of reasons why you need to own a house. This certainly isn't all of them but here are three main reasons.

Number one, God wants you to be the head and not the tail. If you are renting, you are not in control and you are helping build someone else's wealth instead of your own. We will talk more about this later, but God wants you to be the lender, not the borrower.

Number two, a house is a major tool to build wealth. It is God's will for you to have wealth (Deuteronomy 8:18). He wants you to be well taken care of and be in a position to be a blessing to other people. Not only will your house increase in value over the years, but as you build equity, you can then turn around and use that equity to purchase other properties that can create more money for you!

Number three, a house is an avenue in which you can leave an inheritance for your children - and if done right, your children's children (Proverbs 13:22). Whenever you go home to be with the Lord, you can leave your children a paid for house or houses that they could either live in or profit from.

As of this moment, the average house in America costs $309,000. Unfortunately, many parents aren't living according to God's standards and leaving an inheritance for their grandchildren; they are dying and leaving their children debt and funeral bills. Over the years of pastoring, I have met many adult children scraping together money to cover their parent's funeral. That's just not right and that is not God's will. Can you imagine being able to leave your children, at the very least, several hundred thousand dollars? One way you can do that is simply by having a nice, debt free house.

We're going to start off discovering God's will for our houses in the Old Testament. In Hebrews 8:6, we learn that under the New Covenant, we have a better covenant established upon better promises; so you and I actually have it better than those in the Old Covenant!

The great news is that to have a better covenant, you must have at the very least, the best of what the Old Covenant offered. Under the Old Covenant, salvation wasn't available; the people of God were servants of God - not children. So as we study these scriptures, look at all of them from this perspective: if God would want this for His servants, how much more so for His children?

CHAPTER 3
A BEAUTIFUL HOUSE

Deuteronomy 8:11-14 NKJV
11 "Beware that you do not forget the Lord your God by not keeping His commandments, His judgments, and His statutes which I command you today, 12 lest—when you have eaten and are full, and have built beautiful houses and dwell in them; 13 and when your herds and your flocks multiply, and your silver and your gold are multiplied, and all that you have is multiplied; 14 when your heart is lifted up, and you forget the Lord your God.

Notice verse 12 in which Moses states "...when you have built fine, beautiful and pleasant houses to live in, your flocks multiply and your silver and gold multiply and all you have is multiplied..." This doesn't sound like a trailer park! Now I'm not being negative against a mobile home; if you like that, then go for it. I grew up in a mobile home and let me tell you something: living in a 16 foot wide metal box on wheels was not God's best for me!

I don't know how you can read Deuteronomy 8 and think

that God wants you poor! I grew up poor; we were so poor we were actually "po!" I know that probably doesn't translate well in other countries, but if you have been "po" then you know what I'm talking about! God is a master builder and He uses gold, diamonds and other jewels for building materials; do you really think He has a problem if you have some marble floors?

> **Deuteronomy 8:12 NKJV**
> **Lest when you have eaten and are full, and have built beautiful houses and dwell in them.**

God said, "When you build beautiful houses..." Number one, he said "houses" not shacks. God doesn't want His most prized possession living in a dump. It doesn't look good on a parent when their children are not well taken care of. Lacy and I have done our best to make sure Jake always has the best clothes; we don't send him to school with stained, tattered clothes. If his shoes start getting worn down, we go get him a new pair. Why? Because I don't want people to look at him and think negatively of us; how Jake lives is a reflection of us!

> **Deuteronomy 8:11-14 NLT**
> **11 "But that is the time to be careful! Beware that in your plenty you do not forget the Lord your God and disobey his commands, regulations, and decrees that I am giving you today. 12 For when you have become full and prosperous and have built fine homes to live in, 13 and when your flocks and herds have become very large and your silver and gold have multiplied along with everything else, be careful! 14 Do not become proud at that time and forget the Lord your God, who rescued you from slavery in the land of Egypt.**

A Beautiful House

Number two, notice God said, "Houses" not house. God doesn't have a problem with you having multiple houses. It is no different than you having multiple cars, multiple televisions or multiple pairs of pants. Why is it that having two pairs of pants isn't excessive but having two houses is excessive? The only difference is the dollar amount.

The same excuse people would use on the second house, you could use on the second pair of pants or fifth pair of shoes! "The money you spent on the extra one could have been used to help the poor." Don't you realize I can help the poor and have two houses? That's just people's small mindedness. I lost count how many pairs of shoes Lacy has! Does she "need" all of those shoes? She would probably say yes and most ladies would agree. How many guys have multiple guns, fishing rods, etc? Lacy walked in the garage and saw that I had several gas containers and asked why I had so many? I said, "Because I need them!"

If you have a problem with multiple houses, then you should have a problem with multiple anything else! The fact of the matter is that God doesn't have an issue with it at all. From a wealth building standpoint, your house is an investment; it is an avenue of generating wealth for His Kingdom.

Number three, God said "Beautiful houses." He wants you to have a beautiful house! Four posts and a tin roof would be sufficient but that isn't up to God's standards for His children.

BELIEVING GOD FOR A HOUSE

Look at the Message Translation of this passage.

> **Deuteronomy 8:11-14 MSG**
> **11-16 Make sure you don't forget God, your God, by not keeping his commandments, his rules and regulations that I command you today. Make sure that when you eat and are satisfied, build pleasant houses and settle in, see your herds and flocks flourish and more and more money come in, watch your standard of living going up and up—make sure you don't become so full of yourself and your things that you forget God, your God.**

God doesn't have a problem with you having lots of businesses, lots of money, lots of houses and your standard of living continuing to go up and up. What God does have a problem with is that in the midst of your prospering financially and materially, you focus on yourself and you forget about the One who made it all possible! *He doesn't have a problem with what is in your hand as long as it doesn't replace what is in your heart - HIM!*

God is fine with you having all those things; in reality, He wants you to have those things. God just doesn't want you to forget about Him. So get rid of that trash you heard about God wanting you broke and barely getting by. Throw that trash out to the curb! God wants you blessed in every way including a nice beautiful paid for house!

Do you know why God doesn't have a problem with you having nice stuff? First of all, it makes Him look good. What a better way to show that He is a good Father than for His kids to be well taken care of. Second, God doesn't have a problem with you having multiple properties because it puts you in a position to be a blessing to other people. If someone needs a house, you have a spare one to give away or at least house someone for a while if they need it. Third, anytime you buy real estate, you are taking away from Satan's domain and reclaiming it for God!

Friends, the Church should be the biggest real estate owners on the planet. *As a Christian, we should be taking back the earth; not just in authority, but literally the dirt itself.* We should own it instead of the devil owning it! Do you realize that every time you buy a piece of property, you are taking property from the kingdom of darkness and bringing that property over into the Kingdom of God?

Finally, when you own your own home, it helps build your wealth. Real estate has proven over time to be one of the safest and yet surest ways to grow your wealth. You spend a lot of money on a car, but as soon as you drive it off of the car lot, it starts depreciating in value. Basically, when you buy that piece of metal on wheels, you lose money; however, when you buy a house, in almost every case, you start making money!

God is the one who said to build big beautiful houses - just don't forget Him while you are enjoying it. Don't think you are the one who provided the house, the money and the wealth. Why? Because God is the one who gave you the power, ability and blessing to do it.

> **Deuteronomy 8:18 AMP**
> **But you shall remember [with profound respect] the Lord your God, for it is He who is giving you power to make wealth, that He may confirm His covenant which He swore (solemnly promised) to your fathers, as it is this day.**

Like I stated earlier, God wants you to have wealth - so He gave you the power to make wealth! One of the proven ways you can make wealth is through real estate. You can buy a house and over time, build equity, sell it and increase your wealth. If you have multiple houses, you can rent them and increase your wealth even more! The average US home typically appreciates in value 5%-10%. Depending on the area, sometimes that percentage can be much, much higher. With that said, this means the typical house should double in value every 10 years! For the average American, this is the number one avenue of capital growth. Now imagine if you owned several houses or multi door properties that are not only increasing in value but also bringing in monthly revenue!

Think Bigger

We must increase our small thinking. If you have small thinking, you will ask and believe God for small. I like something Dr. Jesse Duplantis says about our asking. He says, "Don't ask God for what you need; ask Him for what you want because your want encompasses the need." Kenneth E. Hagin always said, "Don't limit God with your need. Find out what you need and then ask for extra."

This is the reason the body of Christ is so far behind where we should be in the area of business and finance. Instead of focusing on how we can obtain real estate, build businesses and increase our wealth, we're focusing on how to borrow the money or come up with the best fundraising ideas. We are not focused on thriving; we are focused on surviving. If you are renting, instead of just believing for rent money, start believing for down payment money! If you are in a run down house, instead of asking for money to fix it up, start believing for money to not only fix it up, but money to buy a better house and then rent out the fixer upper.

It's absolutely impossible to read what God has to say about wealth and in this particular case, houses, and yet still walk away thinking small - you have to purposely disregard what God has said in His Word.

The Head And Not The Tail

Deuteronomy 28:8-13 NLT
8 "The Lord will guarantee a blessing on everything you do and will fill your storehouses with grain. The Lord your God will bless you in the land he is giving you. 9 "If you obey the commands of the Lord your God and walk in his ways, the Lord will establish you as his holy people as he swore he would do. 10 Then all the nations of the world will see that you are a people claimed by the Lord,

and they will stand in awe of you. 11 "The Lord will give you prosperity in the land he swore to your ancestors to give you, blessing you with many children, numerous livestock, and abundant crops.12 The Lord will send rain at the proper time from his rich treasury in the heavens and will bless all the work you do. You will lend to many nations, but you will never need to borrow from them. 13 If you listen to these commands of the Lord your God that I am giving you today, and if you carefully obey them, the Lord will make you the head and not the tail, and you will always be on top and never at the bottom.

Deuteronomy 28:8-13 TLB
8 The Lord will bless you with good crops and healthy cattle, and prosper everything you do when you arrive in the land the Lord your God is giving you. 9 He will change you into a holy people dedicated to himself; this he has promised to do if you will only obey him and walk in his ways. 10 All the nations in the world shall see that you belong to the Lord, and they will stand in awe. 11 "The Lord will give you an abundance of good things in the land, just as he promised: many children, many cattle, and abundant crops. 12 He will open to you his wonderful treasury of rain in the heavens, to give you fine crops every season. He will bless everything you do; and you shall lend to many nations, but shall not borrow from them. 13 If you will only listen and obey the commandments of the Lord your God that I am giving you today, he will make you the head and not the tail, and you shall always have the upper hand.

God said He will make you the lender and not the borrower; He will make you the head and not the tail! Not only does God want you to have a big nice house, but He wants you to be the owner and be debt free! He wants you to have a big beautiful house, filled with lots of beautiful things and all of it debt free.

A Beautiful House

We shouldn't be pulling up into our house that is technically owned by the bank and then walking into the house and sitting on the couch that was bought by Visa and watching the TV that was bought with Mastercard, washing our clothes in the washer bought by Discover and sleeping in the bed bought with American Express. There is no way you can relax in a place like that because when you owe, it's a burden on your back. If you lost your job and couldn't make the payments for a few months, they could take your house and take your stuff!

Not only that, if you are renting, you don't even have a say in what the inside or outside of your house looks like. You can't choose to paint it or decorate it without someone else's permission. There are many places that you can't have a pet goldfish because they don't allow any pets. In some places, you can't even hang up a poster on the wall without permission!

Granted, there is a time and place for renting. If the situation you are in is temporary or short term, it doesn't make sense to purchase a house unless you can walk into it with some instant equity. However, if you are going to be in a place for at least five years, I say buy something!

If you are renting, you aren't building wealth; you are building someone else's wealth. Every rent payment, you are increasing someone else and you are staying the same. Again, for temporary or short term situations, renting is the better financial decision in most cases; however, don't get caught in that long term. If you are renting or you owe a mortgage, you are the borrower; you are the tail. God wants you to be the lender; God wants you to be the head.

Your Age Is Not A Factor

There is another issue of small thinking I want to tackle as well. Notice God didn't say anything about your age in any of this. God didn't say you couldn't have a house until you were in your late twenties or thirties nor did He say you couldn't have your house paid for until you are seventy years old! We have bought into a bunch of lies in our society that you can't have something nice and be debt free until you are old and gray.

We are told, "Go get a 30 year mortgage, make your payments and by the time you retire and pay for that house three times because of interest, then you can be debt free." Of course, this isn't counting the people who take out a second mortgage on their house to remodel the house and maybe purchase a new bass boat too. These people they are paying until their physical bodies can barely move and maybe just maybe, the mortgage is paid off before they take their last breath.

Don't tell me that your age is an excuse. Lacy and I have been talking to our son Jake for years about what kind of house he will buy when he graduates high school. We are preparing him at an early age to start thinking big and beyond what is normal. Instead of thinking about a car, why not have your kids already thinking about generating wealth while they are in high school? Most Christians are not thinking this way; most Christians are thinking on a very limited scale and have bought into what is normal in the world.

This is not in the Bible but it is what people have bought into, especially here in America. You have people fresh out of college that get married, buy new cars on credit, get a large mortgage on a house and try to get in one month on credit what it took their parents or grandparents thirty years to get. You can have the nice stuff, but don't limit yourself to thinking that the only way you can have it young is by having debt up to your eyeballs. If that is you, don't get mad at me! Get inspired to get out of that mess and do it God's way!

God never came up with a 30 year mortgage. Man came up with that. Do you know why? Because it makes money off of other people's money. That massive mortgage takes money out of your pocket and puts it many times over into the pockets of evil people when it could be used to be a blessing to other people or at the very least invested to make more money.

Don't Fall Into The Blame Trap

Notice also that God never mentions race, gender or your socioeconomic background. Don't go down the path of using your race or gender as to why you can't own anything. Yes, there are still some racist and prejudiced people in the world, but when you are in Christ, you have an advantage in the world.

> **Deuteronomy 28:13 TLB**
> **13 If you will only listen and obey the commandments of the Lord your God that I am giving you today, he will make you the head and not the tail, and you shall always have the upper hand.**

Don't ever fall into the trap of letting your physical traits or background be a crutch or excuse. No one is holding you back from prospering but you - not the government, not a society, not a people group - no one. Friend, listen to me and listen to me good: Jesus freed you from your excuses. If you want to know why you are not prospering the way God designed and empowered you...look in the mirror and you will find the problem.

God never designed for anyone to be your provider except for Him. If you are blaming a group of people, blaming history, blaming your society, blaming your skin color...stop. All you are doing is revealing to everyone that God is not your source. When God becomes your source, you'll stop blaming others for your lack of progress.

Growing up in the Texas town that I did, I got called all kinds of racial slurs because of my last name. I got into fights because of being Hispanic, told to go back across the Mexican border (even though I'm not even Mexican) and even had a coach that tried to keep me from playing because of my ethnicity. When I was a freshman in high school, I actually had a teacher tell me I wasn't smart enough to make it to college - even though I was in honors classes. On top of that, it didn't help that my family was extremely poor at the time.

My dad had gotten hurt on the job when I was seven years old and it sent us into a downward financial spiral that went out of control. For a good majority of my childhood, we moved from rent house to rent house and even lived with my grandparents for a time. I still remember to this day moving to our mobile home, but having to take sponge baths outside for a few weeks because we didn't have the money to get water run to the mobile home.

Friends, we had it extremely hard financially. I could tell you all kinds of stories: from standing in line with my mom at the food stamp office, watching my mom and dad pawn their wedding rings just so they could pay bills, collecting aluminum cans to recycle for extra cash...my skin color certainly didn't give us any priviledge. I remember all through middle school and high school, going through the lunch line and having to show my "free lunch card" to the cashier while all my friends next to me watched.

There were a lot of things that happened during my school years and I could have allowed them to be an excuse as to why I couldn't do something with my life; sadly, it didn't change once I became an adult. While I went to Bible school, for two years I worked the overnight shift at the homeless shelter; when I got off work, I stood in line with the homeless people for breakfast and then when I came into work at night, I ate their leftover dinner for my dinner.

I could have blamed my ancestry. I could have blamed my last name. I could have blamed the racist people around me. I could have blamed the socioeconomic status of my family and the generations before them, but I refused to. I began to find out in the Bible that God didn't use them as an excuse for my prosperity and His plans for my life. God never mentioned anything about my physical makeup or financial past as a hindrance to me experiencing His will in Heaven in my life on the earth.

Faith Is The Great Equalizer

Friends, faith is the great equalizer. It equals everything out for every single one of us! It doesn't matter how you grew up. Yes, I understand on the natural side of things, every single one of us grew up in different homes with different family situations. People like me grew up dirt poor and in families where no one had ever gone to college before; other people grew up in very wealthy, privileged homes. Some because of skin color or ethnicity may have had some more difficult challenges than others, but I'm telling you, faith will equal out everything.

It doesn't matter how you started out in this natural life because when you grab hold of the Word of God by faith, it can take you to the same place as your wealthy friends...and then past that if you will believe and be led by the Holy Spirit. You may not have their parent's education, wealth and upbringing, but you have faith and you have God's promises; however, the first thing you have got to do is stop making excuses.

Christians should not be making excuses for who they are, what they don't have and what they can't do. In my house, *can't* is a four-letter curse word. We don't say "I can't have this" or "I can't do that" because we can do all things through Christ who gave us strength and I can have whatever I believe and say.

In my late twenties, I began to discover God wanted me to prosper and that I didn't have to live rent house to rent house and barely scrape by. My age, ethnicity, race, economic status, education - none of those things mattered to God because He was my Provider and He would be the one to give me a house among many other things.

CHAPTER 4
A HOUSE FILLED WITH NICE THINGS

Deuteronomy 6:10-12 AMP
10 "Then it shall come about when the Lord your God brings you into the land which He swore (solemnly promised) to [give] your fathers—to Abraham, Isaac, and Jacob—to give you, [a land with] great and splendid cities which you did not build, 11 and houses full of all good things which you did not fill, and hewn (excavated) cisterns (wells) which you did not dig out, and vineyards and olive trees which you did not plant, and you eat and are full and satisfied, 12 then [e]beware that you do not forget the Lord who brought you out of the land of Egypt, out of the house of slavery.

Did you see this? Houses full of good things you did not fill and a supply that you didn't have to supply for yourself. This is the total opposite of the beggar and victim mentality in our world! This right here is the Kingdom mentality - He is the King and He takes care of me! Not only are we reminded here that God wants us to have nice things, particularly a home, we also find out God doesn't want your house empty -

He wants it filled with nice stuff! Not only does He want it filled with nice stuff, He wants those things paid for in full.

Friend, it is not God's will for you to be struggling to get a house and then have to "rent to own" your couch. No! God said He would fill it with good things. Remember that God gives us the power to get wealth and adds no sorrow or anxiety with it.

God wants your house to be filled with good things; He wants you to have beautiful on the outside and beautiful on the inside. He wants you to be able to walk in your house and experience peace, satisfaction and relaxation. He doesn't want you opening your refrigerator to get food and then wondering how you are going to make the refrigerator payment!

God said He would give you large and beautiful cities, which you did not build and houses full of good things, which you did not fill. Don't tell me that what you can have is based on what you make. Come on! Your paycheck does not determine what you can have; your paycheck does not determine what you can do - your faith determines that!

> **Proverbs 24:3-4 NKJV**
> **Through wisdom a house is built and by understanding it is established; By knowledge the rooms are filled with all precious and pleasant riches.**
>
> **Proverbs 24:3-4 AMP**
> **Through skillful and godly Wisdom is a house (a life, a home, a family) built, and by understanding it is**

established [on a sound and good foundation], And by knowledge shall its chambers [of every area] be filled with all precious and pleasant riches.

Proverbs 24:3-4 MSG
It takes wisdom to build a house, and understanding to set it on a firm foundation. It takes knowledge to furnish its rooms with fine furniture and beautiful draperies.

In Proverbs 24:3-4, God tells us it is by knowledge that every room of our house is filled with precious and pleasant riches. The Message translation says, "Rooms filled with fine furniture and beautiful draperies." Friend, putting aluminum foil on your windows to keep the heat out and eyes looking in - that's not what God is talking about! I drove by a house the other day that had a towel hanging outside over the front window and attached with duct tape! That is not the goodness of God in the land of the living - that is poverty and not God's will for your house.

Psalm 112:3 NIV
Wealth and riches are in their houses, and their righteousness endures forever.

For a long time, Lacy and I went through a period of hand me down furniture and buying stuff either in garage sales or on credit. Thankfully, Lacy is a great shopper and bargainer; she got us some tremendous finds over the years in filling our house with some nice things, but thank God, He has even better! I shouldn't have to buy a refrigerator that has a big ding on the front because of the discount or buying a couch that has mismatched legs or getting a washer and dryer with rust on it because I can't buy a new one.

I don't know if you realize it or not, but you get what you pay for. Just because it is cheap doesn't mean it is a good deal. I may get it cheap but if it breaks next year and I have to buy another, in most cases I will have spent more money in the long run.

I will never forget the first house God gave us that started our journey of prosperity. It was a Heaven deal but it took a wonderful friend to loan us $3,000 in order to buy it. It was a large house on eleven acres of land; my biggest problem was that I didn't have a lawn mower much less a riding mower to cut all of that grass. All I had was a weed eater! I didn't have any money for a mower, so every day, I would go outside and use my weed eater to cut about ¼ of an acre around our house - I was always weeding and did that for an entire summer! I can honestly tell you though that I never complained. I was so thankful for our house and the land; I was thanking God for the opportunity to cut all that grass with my weed eater, but I was also thanking Him for a mower!

I started looking online and found a guy selling his used riding mower for $400. By that time I had saved up just enough and was able to buy it from him - but it was a dumb decision. It was old but it was all I could afford. I took it home and it lasted me about 3 months; one day it started backfiring and smoking and just stopped. I didn't know whether to cry or scream. If I simply would have waited just a little longer, I could have saved up more money and bought a more dependable mower, but I decided to go cheap and it ended up being an expensive decision later on.

Stop Thinking Small

Stop thinking small. It is not God's will for you to have a dryer that has to do one load five times to get it dry! It is not God's will for your mattress to be so old that when you lay in it, it feels like a hammock! Believe me, Lacy and I had one of those. Our first mattress was a hand me down that was handed down after 20 years! It was so worn down, you couldn't sleep in the middle because it had a cavity in it. If you happened to roll over to the middle of the bed, you might need a rope to help pull you out! However, we were excited to move from our old full size bed to our 20 year old king size bed with the cavity. It was an upgrade...barely...but we were grateful.

Thankfully, we have moved beyond those days. Now, we have a super nice bed that we can actually control the settings with our phone and choose how firm or soft we want it. I have mine set at 55 and Lacy has her side set to 40. Before, we would constantly wake up with sore backs and unrested; now, we sleep better than ever before. Why? Good things in our house!

Proverbs 24:3-4 AMP
3 Through skillful and godly Wisdom is a house (a

life, a home, a family) built, and by understanding it is established [on a sound and good foundation], 4 And by knowledge shall its chambers [of every area] be filled with all precious and pleasant riches.

I love that God tells us He wants every room filled with all precious and pleasant riches. That doesn't sound like a "bless them a little bit" type of God does it? God wants you to not only pull up into your driveway and say "The Lord is good!" but in every room you walk in, you should be saying "Good God!" Some people don't understand it, but this brings God glory. It brings Him glory when He sees His children blessed and other people recognize it as well.

1 Kings 10:1-5 MSG
The queen of Sheba heard about Solomon and his connection with the Name of God. She came to put his reputation to the test by asking tough questions. She made a grand and showy entrance into Jerusalem—camels loaded with spices, a huge amount of gold, and precious gems. She came to Solomon and talked about all the things that she cared about, emptying her heart to him. Solomon answered everything she put to him—nothing stumped him. When the queen of Sheba experienced for herself Solomon's wisdom and saw with her own eyes the palace he had built, the meals that were served, the impressive array of court officials and sharply dressed waiters, the lavish crystal, and the elaborate worship extravagant with Whole-Burnt-Offerings at the steps leading up to The Temple of God, it took her breath away.

The Queen of Sheba was blown away when she saw how nice Solomon's palace was, how well dressed his staff were and even the lavish meals and plates they were served on! It literally took her breath away and she passed out!

I want you to notice a few things in this story. First of all, do we see anywhere where God had a problem with the lavishness of Solomon's palace and the things that were in it? Absolutely not. God never admonished Solomon and told him that all of his material things and the house he built was excessive. Actually, it was the wisdom of Solomon, the excessiveness of his palace and everything in it that caused the Queen of Sheba to bless the Lord!

Never Apologize for The Goodness Of God

Second, notice that Solomon did not apologize for his wealth or all of the material things he had. Friend, don't you ever apologize or be embarrassed of the blessings of God in your life. You should never be ashamed of the goodness of God that you are enjoying. Remember, God is the one who gave you the power to get wealth - not you. It's the blessing of the Lord that makes one rich! God did it; not you!

We should never downplay what God has done. You should never feel like you need to hide something God has given you because of someone else's opinion. If they are mad because you have it or offended because of what God has done for them, well they can just deal with it. God loves to lavishly and excessively bless His children with good things; however, if you are offended at what someone has, rest assured you won't have it. Always guard yourself of offense when someone else is blessed. Don't curse them; rejoice with them! Be happy for them and start shouting, "I'm next!"

When God has been good to you, it's not a time to hide it; it is a time to celebrate it and put it on display. Some people would call that pride; I call it a testimony! I find it interesting that in 1 Chronicles 29, we find David preparing all the materials for the temple. Then David blatantly tells everyone that he personally was giving over two billion dollars of his own wealth towards the building of the temple! He wasn't ashamed of it. It wasn't pride. It wasn't bragging. This was a testimony of God's goodness!

We are the ones who have looked at things like that as pride. Do you know why? Because too many people get offended at seeing the good things God has done for other people and start questioning, "Well what about me? Where is my stuff?"

There will always be people like that and I guarantee, the more you begin to prosper and walk according to God's principles of finance, you will find more and more haters - but don't worry about them. Keep your heart right towards God and people. Keep praising Him for what He has done and all He is going to do.

Every time you walk through your house, every room you

go in, you should find something to praise Him for! We should also get to the point that when people come into our house, they see the goodness of God to such a degree, it will cause them to praise God too!

CHAPTER 5
A SAFE HOUSE

Isaiah 32:18 MSG
My people will live in a peaceful neighborhood - in safe houses, in quiet gardens.

God not only wants you to live in a beautiful home that you own and filled with good things, He also wants you to live in a safe neighborhood. It is not God's will for you to be living in a place where bullets are flying through your yard. It is not God's will for you to live in a place that you can't even walk down the road safely and enjoy a cool evening breeze.

Notice the words *peaceful* and *secure* in Isaiah 32:18. God wants your home to be a place of rest. You shouldn't be at home worrying about the safety of your children while they play outside; it hurts my heart to see people have to live like that. I remember when I was in 5th grade, our rent house wasn't in the best part of town. When the street lights came on, that was our sign to go inside!

BELIEVING GOD FOR A HOUSE

The other day I was watching television and on the broadcast they were interviewing some kids in Chicago. The kids said they can't even go outside and play because they are scared of getting shot. One of the young teenagers said there are always gang fights in the area and guns being fired. They then interviewed one of the parents and the mother stated she was trying to homeschool her kids out of fear for their safety in walking to school.

If you live in a bad neighborhood, let that be your sign: this is not God's best for me. It's time for you to move on up! Back in the 1980's, one of my favorite TV shows was *The Jeffersons*. I really liked George because he just told it like it was. But just like the Jeffersons, it is time for you to move on up to the East side! Now where you live, the other side might be the best side - but you get my point. God doesn't have a problem with you upgrading.

If what we are experiencing is not the will of Heaven on Earth, then it's time to move on. Let's grab hold of the Word of God by faith and move on up! Let's go up to God's standard for His kids. Your home should be a place of solitude that after a long day of work, you can come home, kick off your shoes and relax in the place God gave you. Your home should be peaceful, not stressful!

CHAPTER 6
A BIG HOUSE

Psalm 18:19 NIV
He brought me out into a spacious place; he rescued me because he delighted in me.

In addition to God wanting us to have a beautiful paid for house, filled with nice things and located in a safe, peaceful neighborhood, God also wants it to be big. Now granted, big is different for almost everyone. For some people, a 1200 sq ft house is big; for others, small is 3,000 sq ft or even 10,000 sq ft. You'll never find where God puts a limit on the square footage of your house; that is totally dependent on you.

Psalm 18:19 says He also brought me out into a broad place, a spacious place, a large place, a big place...God size! God doesn't want you being cramped; He doesn't want you cooped up!

Up until I was seven years old, our family was doing decent financially. My dad was working for Mobile Oil Refineries in

Beaumont, TX at the time, but I remember one day, my mom got a call and we had to rush to the hospital. My dad had an accident at his job and had broke his ankle, knee and injured his back. On that day, my mom was 27 years old, my dad was 32 years old and our life radically changed for the worse.

Neither one of my parents had a college education at the time (no one on either side had ever been to college.) My mom hadn't been working the entire time because she was at home taking care of me and my two siblings.

My dad was unable to work for almost five years and my mom was selling perfume at Dillards for minimum wage. From the time I was seven years old until I was fourteen years old, we moved ten times within a twenty mile radius. For a while, it seemed like every six months we were moving to another place. We went to several rent houses, moved in with my grandparents twice...we got really good at packing a moving truck!

A Stolen Bike And Cockroaches For Roommates

I remember the first place we moved to after my dad got hurt; it was a small apartment at Country Village Apartments in Cheek, TX. Things had immediately gotten bad since we had little income and had to sell our house and move into an apartment; however, after only a few days, it got even worse.

You see, I had one of those pedal bikes that once you got

going really fast, you could pull a lever, lock up the wheels and do a spin out. We didn't have room for it in the house, so I would just leave it on our little porch outside the front door. Only a short time into our new journey, someone stole my bike. Someone stole my wheels and I had no transportation! I was one mad seven year old!

After a few days, it got even worse - the cockroaches started getting bold and moving in. You would open the kitchen cabinet and a few would crawl out. Lift up the couch cushion and one would say "Hello!" It seemed like everywhere we turned, there would be a cockroach or two. Then one night, all the cockroaches from hell made their way into our apartment.

Myself, my brother and sister were sharing a room and my brother and I had bunk beds. I slept in the top bunk and on this one particular night, I felt something fall onto my face. It was dark in the room so I could only see a little with the moonlight that was seeping through our bedroom window. I brushed off my face and tried to go back to sleep. Then I felt something again fall onto my face, but this time I felt it move. I looked up at the ceiling, which was two feet from my face, and I could see something dark moving on the ceiling. I reached up and touch it, *but it wasn't an it...it was a them!* It was a massive pile of cockroaches walking all over our ceiling and then they started falling all over me.

I started screaming and my parents came running into the

room and cut on the lights. It seemed like every cockroach in the city had showed up in my room and called all their family and friends for a party! One thing you have to understand about Texas cockroaches - they are big and they fly and they were everywhere! After that night, it wasn't even a discussion - it was time to move again!

I remember when i was in sixth grade, we moved into this two bedroom apartment in Lumberton, Texas - and it was small. Me, my brother and my sister were sharing a room; it was more like a closet! My brother and I still were sharing our bunk beds and my sister had a twin mattress on the floor. This room was so small that with our bunk bed and her mattress in the room, there was maybe a foot of space to walk in between them. To get from the door to the window in between the beds, you basically had to turn sideways and shuffle your feet! You talk about being cooped up! That's not peaceful; that is stressful. Even though we love family, sometimes you just need some "me space!" Do you know what I'm talking about? Sometimes you need to have some space away from the people in your house!

Coops Are For Chickens

Friend, God doesn't want you cooped up. There is a reason we call a chicken's house a chicken coup. Because it is small and those chickens are all cooped up! Do you know what is interesting? Chickens are just dumb, but even being dumb chickens understand this: they don't want to be cooped up!

A Big House

For several years now, we have had chickens along with all of Lacy's other animals. Each morning she goes down to the chicken coop to let them out so they can roam freely. As soon as she opens the door, all those dumb chickens come bursting out of the door and start stretching out and enjoying some wide open spaces! Chickens are stupid but even they know they're not supposed to be cooped up! If a dumb chicken knows that, then we should wake up to that too.

Remember, God said, "I'm bringing them out into a broad, large, expansive place!" God wants you and your family to have lots of room and not be cramped!

Enlarge Your Tent

Deuteronomy 28:8-13 TLB
10 All the nations in the world shall see that you belong to the Lord, and they will stand in awe. 11 "The Lord will give you an abundance of good things in the land, just as he promised: many children, many cattle, and abundant crops. 12 He will open to you his wonderful treasury of rain in the heavens, to give you fine crops every season. He will bless everything you do; and you shall lend to many nations, but shall not borrow from them. 13 If you will only listen and obey the commandments of the Lord your God that I am giving you today, he will make you the head and not the tail, and you shall always have the upper hand.

In verse 11, God said He is going to grant you plenty of good things. You can't have a small house with a small patch of land and hold plenty of good things. Even back in Bible days, the vast majority of the people were farmers and ranchers. You can't have a large amount of crops and a large amount of cattle and yet live on ¼ acre lot! Believe me! Lacy has several horses, miniature donkeys, goats, chickens, ducks… we currently have eleven acres of land to not only accommodate us but also the animals!

God doesn't want you to have small; He wants you to have big because He is a big God! If God wanted to, He could have made Heaven small and have all of us living in subsidized studio apartments with community showers! No, God's idea was for every single one of us to have a mansion - and if God is okay with me having a mansion in Heaven, He must be okay with me having a mansion on earth. You may say, "Yes, but I live in the city and it is more expensive in the city than it is in the country." Well, it is more expensive in the city than in the country, but where in the Bible did God mention your bank account as a factor? Some cities are more expensive to live in than other cities, but where did God mention location? God never talks about price; He talks about provision!

When Jesus was on earth, He prayed, "Father, Your will be done on Earth as it is in Heaven" (Matthew 6:10.) You will never find where God does things small! If you have a small place, you can only hold a small amount of stuff and if you have a small amount of stuff, you can only be a blessing to a small amount of people. Remember, Biblical prosperity is not just about you having stuff; it's about you being in a position that you are so blessed, you can be a blessing to other people. You can not only show the goodness of God in your personal life, but you can manifest the goodness of God in other people's lives!

Isaiah 65:23 KJV
They shall build houses and inhabit them; They shall plant vineyards and eat their fruit.

How are you going to build a vineyard on a small lot of land? How are you going to have a farm? God was talking to agricultural people here and even they knew they couldn't do that with just a little bitty house on a little bitty piece of land.

I don't know about you, but I like my space and I like my privacy. If I can look out my bathroom window and talk to my neighbor in their bathroom window, that's too close for me! If it is too close for a chicken, it's too close for me; I know I'm smarter than a chicken! I know some people that love living in skyrise condos and apartment buildings right in the city; they don't want to mess with cutting grass! If that's you, then go for it, but instead of owning a large parcel of land, own the entire building!

Deuteronomy 6:10-12 MSG
When God, your God, ushers you into the land he promised through your ancestors Abraham, Isaac, and Jacob to give you, you're going to walk into large, bustling cities you didn't build, well-furnished houses you didn't buy, come upon wells you didn't dig, vineyards and olive orchards you didn't plant. When you take it all in and settle down, pleased and content, make sure you don't forget how you

BELIEVING GOD FOR A HOUSE

got there—God brought you out of slavery in Egypt.

Remember: God wants you to have a beautiful house in a nice, safe neighborhood that you can be proud of. He wants you to have a house that has plenty of room for you and your family, filled with nice things and everything paid for.

God doesn't have a problem with you having a couple of couches and nice paintings and pictures on the walls and stuff in your refrigerator. He wants you to have a nice bed with as many pillows that you want! He wants you to have stuff in your house!

And don't forget what God said in Deuteronomy 28. He said He's going to bless you abundantly. God doesn't have a problem with you having material things like other people do. I've had people tell me, "That house is just too expensive." "That house is too big." "Why do you need two refrigerators and two dishwashers in your kitchen?" You will never hear God say, "Too big or too much!"

The problem with people who think something is too big, too expensive or unnecessary for you is that they can't see themselves having it so they don't think you should have it. They can't see themselves moving beyond their two bedroom/one bathroom house even though they have five people living in it and they know they need more room. They can't see themselves having a larger house with a few extra bedrooms for guests and maybe a spare guest house on their property that they could rent out for some extra money.

Stop listening to small minded people that can't even see themselves having it. Just keep your eyes and ears on God's Word. God says He wants you to have something good. He wants you to have something beautiful. God's standards far exceed the standards of men.

CHAPTER 7
A DEBT FREE HOUSE

Deuteronomy 28:12-13 NKJV
12 You shall lend to many nations, but you shall not borrow. 13 And the Lord will make you the head and not the tail; you shall be above only, and not be beneath, if you heed the commandments of the Lord your God, which I command you today, and are careful to observe them.

God didn't come up with the idea of the government or banks giving you and I a loan so that we can have a house. Remember, you and I we were born of God and sent from Heaven into this Earth. It was God's mission for you and I to come here, do a job and then send Jesus to bring us back home. He did not send you and I to the Earth to live from the Earth; He sent us here to represent Him and live from Heaven.

In John 17:18, Jesus said, "In the same way you sent Me, I am sending them." *God never sends you on a mission in which you are dependent on the world for provision.* Remember Philippians 4:19? My God shall supply all my needs - not the bank, not the government, not your family, etc. God will do it.

BELIEVING GOD FOR A HOUSE

Yes there are many channels, but there is only one Source.

Some would say, "Well why can't a bank be a channel?" Well, a bank could certainly be a place to get money; the problem is, they can tell you what to do with it. They tell you how much interest you will pay and how long you have to pay it. Now I'm certainly not saying that borrowing money from a bank is a sin. God wouldn't tell us to be the lender instead of the borrower if borrowing was wrong. There are times in which you can borrow money and use that debt to actually make money, especially in the area of real estate; you just have to remember that in any situation in which you are the borrower, you are not the head in that situation. There is nothing wrong with using the world's system, but let's continue to grow so that we get to the point we are entirely independent from it!

Isaiah 65:21-22 NKJV
21 They shall build houses and inhabit them; They shall plant vineyards and eat their fruit. 22 They shall not build and another inhabit; They shall not plant and another eat.

Not only does God's statement in Isaiah 65:21-22 apply to His will for you to have a large house, it also applies to His will that your home be debt free. If you have a mortgage, essentially, you don't actually own your house until the loan is paid in full. Do you understand that? Say you bought a house for $200,000 and over twenty five years, you had paid $190,000. If you missed three payments, even after all those years of making all those paymenst, they could take the house from you and you would have nothing despite all the money you had paid. Until that loan is paid for, they are the head and you are the tail. I know many people who have built homes, paid on those homes for years and then because of a sickness or losing a job, they ended up being foreclosed on by the bank and losing their home.

Lacy and I were unfortunately in that situation many years ago. We had a business in which someone was stealing money from us and eventually we lost our business that led to us losing our home. That was an experience I would wish on no one. It's a horrible thing to get a letter in the mail stating you have two weeks to vacate your home and then one day to find the locks changed and a sign on the door stating it is now owned by the bank. That was one of the lowest days of my life - not including the days after when we had creditors showing up at our door to collect and we would run, hide in a room and cut off the lights until they left!

Proverbs 33:3 AMP
The curse of the Lord is on the house of the wicked, but He blesses the home of the just and righteous.

Friend, God doesn't want us going thirty years being a slave to someone. We have to stop looking to people and entities to be our source. Although I am thankful for the avenues out there to help us achieve our goals, I don't want to be dependent on a person; whether it be for my health or my finances.

BELIEVING GOD FOR A HOUSE

Isaiah 32:17-18 NLT
17 And this righteousness will bring peace. Yes, it will bring quietness and confidence forever. 18 My people will live in safety, quietly at home. They will be at rest.

God wants you to have a big, beautiful home filled with nice things that no one can take from you. We need to be in a position that if for some reason I lost my job, my first thought is not, "How am I going to make the house note?"

We should be in a position of being debt free so that if some negative situation did come against us, we don't have to worry about such things! It's a good thing emotionally and psychologically to have peace of mind knowing that no matter what goes on in my life, this house is mine and nobody is going to come in here and take it from me.

He wants you to have a big beautiful house, filled with lots of beautiful things and all of it debt free. We shouldn't be pulling up into our house that is technically owned by the bank and then walking into the house and sitting on a chair that is charging you interest, eating at a table that is charging you interest, opening a refrigerator that is charging you interest and sleeping in a bed that is charging you interest.

Every room should not be a reminder that you owe; it should be a reminder that you own! If you lost your job and couldn't make the payments for a few months, they could take your house and take your stuff! Who wants that stress?

A Debt Free House

God Wants You Blessed, Not Stressed

It is a very stressful thing to not be able to take some vacation or miss a few days of work to take care of family because, "I need to work to pay the house and the bills." It's one of the reasons people begin to freak out when the economy starts tanking and people start losing jobs - they immediately think about their house. Shelter and food are two of the most basic essentials of life and God never intended for us to be concerned about either one. However, the vast majority of us get up in the morning and head to work singing, "I owe, I owe, it's off to work I go. Got a house note and all my credit cards, I owe, I owe!"

God doesn't want you stressed; He wants us blessed! He doesn't want us broke; He wants us rich! He doesn't want you bound to a mortgage; He wants you bound to Him! When you are free from a mortgage, you are even more free to be a blessing to other people. Imagine what it would be like to have an extra $1500 or $3000 a month? Imagine the freedom you would experience not having rent or a mortgage?

I can see you right now thinking about it and the peace that immediately comes just at the thought of not having that burden on your shoulders...but that is what God wants you to have every single day of your life. God's plan was never for you to have to wait until you were seventy years old and retired to finally take a breath and enjoy financial freedom. Of course, in today's American society, many people are getting into their retirement age and discovering they don't have enough money to retire!

What if for those last thirty years, instead of having to make a mortgage payment, you were putting that same amount into some type of retirement account or investment? Think about it simply from an investment standpoint. Even if you simply put $1,000 every month into an investment account at 5%...if you did that for thirty years, that comes to over $850,000! You would have that money to invest and also be in a better position to be a blessing to other people.

Can you imagine being in a position that if your friend lost their job, you could relieve stress from them and pay their house note until they were able to start working again? Friend, that's the Kingdom life - that is a life lived with a Kingdom mentality in which we can represent God and be a dispenser of His wealth.

When people are believing God for money, it doesn't rain down out of the sky; God speaks to people and those people are the ones who take of the money God blessed them with and they give it to the one believing for it. God wants you financially free not only for you, but also for others. When you remove the mortgage off of your responsibilities, you automatically position yourself to be an even greater force for God on the earth as an owner, a giver and a wealth creator.

CHAPTER 8
THE SUBSTANCE OF THINGS

Hebrews 11:1 NKJV
Now faith is the substance of things hoped for, the evidence of things not seen.

Faith is the substance of what? Things! Is a couch or bed a thing? Is a car a thing? What about a house? Faith is the substance of things. If you need something, faith is the answer and it is the great equalizer. *Regardless of your background, faith in God will take you past your disadvantages and give you an advantage in life.* Faith in God will also get you the things you need in life.

Regardless of your situation, if you are looking for an excuse as to why you can't have something, I guarantee you will find it; however, once you get your eyes off of the circumstances and on to God, the excuses go away. With faith in God, there is always a way! It doesn't matter if the thing you need is a washing machine or a house itself, faith is the substance of all things hoped for.

Hebrews 11:3 NKJV
By faith we understand that the worlds were framed by the word of God, so that the things which are seen were not made of things which are visible.

God created everything you can see in this world by faith. Friend, God doesn't expect you to live and operate any differently than He does. God is a faith God. He lives by faith, speaks by faith, creates by faith and operates by faith. The entire universe came into existence because God, by faith, spoke it into existence.

We Create The World We Need

In the same manner, we can create the world we need. If you have faith, you can have what you need and nothing in this world can stop you. By faith, we can obtain the material things we need in this world!

There is a way you can get it and it has nothing to do with your physical person; it has everything to do with your authority you have on the earth as a representative of God. You are the believer; God is the performer. If you will put your faith in Him, it will come to pass.

Hebrews 11 isn't the only place we see the relationship between faith and obtaining things. Let's look at what Jesus had to say about faith and things in Mark 11.

> **Mark 11:23-24 NKJV**
> **22 So Jesus answered and said to them, "Have faith in God. 23 For assuredly, I say to you, whoever says to this mountain, 'Be removed and be cast into the sea,' and does not doubt in his heart, but believes that those things he says will be done, he will have whatever he says. 24 Therefore I say to you, whatever things you ask when you pray, believe that you receive them, and you will have them.**

Let's break down this marvelous teaching Jesus gave us. First of all, Jesus said, "Have faith in God." Some translations say, "Have the faith of God or have the God kind of faith." You must understand Jesus was speaking to unsaved people at this time; they didn't have the faith of God because Jesus had not died on the cross and arisen from the dead.

Because of salvation, we have the faith of God because of our union with Jesus! We have the ability and equipment to believe just like Him! So with that proper perspective, look at Jesus explanation of how faith works.

Whoever Says

In verse 23, Jesus states, "Whoever says..." Now, this is where it gets interesting. Jesus didn't say the preacher, the person who has gone to Bible school, the person with ten degrees, or the person making $100,000 a year - Jesus says "whoever."

This one word *whoever* removes all the excuses we give ourselves when it comes to our skin color, our country of origin, our socioeconomic status,etc...Jesus says this is for *whoever*. Are you a *whoever?* Yes you are; therefore, pay attention because Jesus is talking about you!

> **Mark 11:23 NKJV**
> **Whoever says to this mountain, 'Be removed and be cast into the sea,' and does not doubt in his heart, but believes that those things he says will be done, he will have whatever he says.**

Jesus explains how faith works: you believe in your heart and speak what you believe. Believing and speaking is faith in operation. So again, notice there is no mention of your physical makeup nor your physical circumstances. Whoever says - that qualifies everyone. In other words, regardless of the circumstances, if you can believe it, you can have it. If you can believe that the things you say will be done, you will have whatever things you say.

Now this isn't you just making a positive confession; this is you speaking what you seriously believe. A lot of people think this is all about positive thinking and positive confession but it is not. Jesus said in Luke 6:45 that out of the abundance of your heart is what you will speak. If you want to know what you truly believe, watch what comes out of your mouth when pressure comes; *when you get squeezed, your true beliefs come out!*

> **Mark 11:24 NKJV**
> **Therefore I say to you, whatever things you ask when you pray, believe that you receive them, and you will have them.**

Lastly, notice when the receiving of the things takes place; it is not when you see it with your eyes, it is when you receive it by faith. Believe that you have received it - that is when you will have it. This is the operation of faith! Get the Word of God for your situation, believe what He said, declare it and receive it - it is that simple.

The Title Deed

> **Hebrews 11:1 AMP**
> **Now faith is the assurance (title deed, confirmation) of things hoped for (divinely guaranteed), and the evidence of things not seen [the conviction of their reality—faith comprehends as fact what cannot be experienced by the physical senses**

Faith is the title deed of things. Do you know what a title deed does for you? When you have the title to a house, that piece of paper is all the proof you need to prove to anyone that you legally own that house. If I have the title deed, I don't need to see the house to prove that I own the house; that's the purpose of the title!

So when it comes to me believing for a house, faith is my title deed, the confirmation in my heart; it is the evidence of the house I don't see. Remember what Jesus said in Mark 11, "Believe you receive it and you shall have it." When you are living in the house is not when you receive it; when you believe you have it - that is what puts you in the position to see it manifest in the natural.

This is how faith works and what it will do for you. *Remember, faith in God is not only the great equalizer, it is also an excuse eliminator!* Faith (not money, race, genealogy, education) is the substance of the things!

Remember, faith isn't just about making the right confessions; it's about saying what you believe. However, there is another aspect of faith I want to show you by looking at a guy named Abraham.

Romans 4:18-21 NLT
18 Even when there was no reason for hope, Abraham kept hoping—believing that he would become the father of many nations. For God had said to him, "That's how many descendants you will have!" 19 And Abraham's faith did not weaken, even though, at about 100 years of age, he figured his body was as good as dead—and so was Sarah's womb.20 Abraham never wavered in believing God's promise. In fact, his faith grew stronger, and in this he brought glory to God. 21 He was fully convinced that God is able to do whatever he promises.

Fully Convinced

God had promised Abraham that despite being old and Sarah

past the physical age of being able to bear children, God was not only going to make them parents in their old age, but make them the origin of nations. Romans 4 tells us that Abraham never wavered in believing God's promise; he was fully convinced that God would do it. This goes right along with what Jesus said in Mark 11:24, "Believe that you receive it and you shall have it."

For a time, Abraham doubted what God said; at one point, he even laughed it off. It took Abraham some time of renewing his mind to the faithfulness of God. When Abraham counted God faithful and was able to see with his spirit what needed to be seen in the natural, Abraham became fully convinced. Abraham was fully convinced that what God had promised was his - despite the circumstances.

Remember, Abraham and Sarah were both old - past the years of having children. But God! God said that despite their circumstances and despite the impossibility, they would have a natural born child of their own. However, just because God said it did not mean it would automatically come to pass; they had to believe it in order for God to perform it. God willed it. Abraham and Sarah believed it. God performed it.

SECTION TWO

HOW TO RECEIVE YOUR HOUSE

CHAPTER 9
GET YOUR HOPES UP

You need to get your hopes up. I have had people get mad at me and say, "All this faith preaching on money and healing; all you are doing is getting people's hopes up. How dare you!" Well you know what? That's exactly what I am endeavoring to do. I want to get your hopes up! Faith is the substance of things hoped for! If you have no hope, you have nothing to release your faith on! You need to get your hopes up but you can't have your expectation high if you don't know what is available; this is why we started off with 1 John 5:14.

1 John 5:14 NKJV
Now this is the confidence that we have in Him, that if we ask anything according to His will, He hears us.

Once you know what the will of God is concerning your situation, you need to get your hopes up. You need to get your expectation up because now I have something to base my faith on and release my faith on. Let me give you a practical example of this. Lets say that you wanted a pay raise at your job. Would you be confident in asking your boss? A major factor would be in your knowledge.

Faith in God begins where the will of God is known. If you had no idea what your boss would say, your confidence in approaching them would be totally different than if your boss had told you, "Anytime you need a pay raise, come tell me and I will give you one." When we know God's will in a situation, it gives us boldness and assurance that we will receive that which we have believed!

It Is Time To Dream

So once you have the assurance, start dreaming! Start driving through neighborhoods that you would desire to live in. *You have to raise your hopes past where they have been; otherwise, you will never go past where you are.*

I'll never forget when Lacy and I were dating, we would drive through some of the nice neighborhoods in Tulsa and just look at the houses. One time, we went through this beautiful neighborhood and took pictures of the type of houses we liked and would want to live in. Now at that time, I could barely fill up the gas tank of my car, but I was allowing myself to dream.

I was in no position to buy a car, much less a house. While Lacy and I were dating, I got into a car wreck and totaled my car; the only way I was able to get another one was because Lacy loaned me the $500 for the down payment!

I was in such bad financial shape I could barely put gas in my car and I was eating breakfast and dinner at the homeless shelter that I worked at!

Make A Vision Board

Despite all of that, I was dreaming. I was getting my hopes up and for years, we had those pictures on our vision board of what we would one day have (I still have those pictures even after 18 years.) Find the things that make you say "Wow!" and then start renewing your mind and seeing yourself in it.

Friend, you may be in a government apartment or you may be on the other side of the world and living in a hut; regardless, start dreaming and get your hopes up. Get on the internet and start looking at houses. Start dreaming about the layout, the colors you would use and the furniture you would put in it. If you have a house but you are wanting a vacation home or want to own an apartment complex, start looking at them! Cut out pictures from a magazine, print pictures from the internet and put them on a vision board.

What is a vision board? It's a board you put on your wall and post the things you are believing God for. Lacy and I have done this for years. We have pictures of houses, trips, vehicles, projects, etc of things we want to see take place in our lives. Some of them are things I am believing for now and some are things I'm working on simply getting past "The Wow Factor."

You need to do this for your house! Find pictures of things you want and hang them on your board. This allows you to see them with your eyes so you can start seeing yourself with them in your spirit and your mind. Find the house you want and then cut out a picture of you and paste it on the house so you can see yourself in your house! I actually have done that! You do whatever it takes to see yourself in that house. Once you can see it with your mind, that's when you know your soul has hooked up to your spirit and that's when you can release your faith.

Genesis 15:4-6 NLT
4 Then the Lord said to him, "No, your servant will not be your heir, for you will have a son of your own who will be your heir." 5 Then the Lord took Abram outside and said to him, "Look up into the sky and count the stars if you can. That's how many descendants you will have!" 6 And Abram believed the Lord, and the Lord counted him as righteous because of his faith.

Your faith will never rise above your hope and your hope will never rise above your vision. You will never be in a position to believe for it if you can't even see yourself having it. This is why God had Abraham start going out at night and counting the stars.

God wanted Abraham to start visualizing all the descendants

he would have despite the fact he was old and childless. It was the reason God had Abraham look at the sand and visualize all the people that would carry his DNA. *What you put your eyes on will determine what becomes real and normal to you.*

CHAPTER 10
STOP CONSIDERING YOUR CIRCUMSTANCES

The second thing you need to do is you need to stop considering your circumstances and start considering the promises. This is exactly what Abraham had to do.

> **Romans 4:18-19 NLT**
> **18 Even when there was no reason for hope, Abraham kept hoping—believing that he would become the father of many nations. For God had said to him, "That's how many descendants you will have!" 19 And Abraham's faith did not weaken, even though, at about 100 years of age, he figured his body was as good as dead—and so was Sarah's womb.**

Abraham stopped considering the circumstances that it was impossible and started considering the promise because God all things are possible. In the same way, you need to stop looking at how much money you make you and stop looking at the economic conditions of your country. God isn't moved by your paycheck or government interest rates. We may live in this world, but we are not of this world.

You need to get your hopes up but it will never happen with your eyes on the circumstances. You can not do the possible in God while looking at the impossibilities of man; yet this is exactly why so many Christians don't see results and wonder why. *It's because they are saying the right things while looking at the wrong things*; as a result, they don't believe what they are saying because what they see is more real to them than what God said.

Get Past The Wow Factor

You need to get past "The Wow Factor." Do you know what the Wow Factor is? The Wow Factor is when you see something so nice, your eyes get big, your heart starts racing and your jaw drops as you say, "Wow!" *As long as you are "wowing," you won't be believing.* Do you know why? Because in the wow stage, that thing is bigger to you than God.

When I was a teenager, our family vehicle was an eighties model Chevy Blazer that we called "The Brown Dog." It was brown with white rusted steel rims and had plastic where the back window was supposed to be - all connected with gray duct tape! On top of that, it had a rusted out hole in the back right above the exhaust pipe; as long as you were driving, you were fine, but as soon as you came to a stop light, you needed a

Stop Considering Your Circumstances

gas mask! You didn't want to be sitting there too long without moving or the exhaust fumes started filling the truck!

Given our financial situation during my childhood, there weren't too many things that didn't make me say "Wow!" Growing up, I thought the only way we could have something nice was if we won it in the lottery or something like that.

I distinctly remember as a kid going with my mom and siblings to a car lot for a giveaway near Sam's Club in Beaumont, Texas. They were giving away this small red car; it wasn't anything fancy but it was way better than what we were driving. My mom filled out the card and put it in the basket along with the hundreds of other people that were there. I remember hoping and wishing we would win that car but we didn't. I figured maybe another giveaway would come around and maybe we could win one. I had no clue God not only wanted us to have a car and a house but would also give us one too! I had a poverty mindset that had to be changed.

I had to fight to get over the Wow Factor; the too big factor, the too much, too expensive factor. As long as you are saying "Wow!" you are saying, "I can't ever see myself having that." Friend, you have to get past that. If getting your first house seems impossible, that is what you need to work on first. Forget about the down payment - work on renewing your mind and begin seeing what seems big to seem small. If you need a bigger house but it seems like, with all the family expenses, it would never be possible, that is your first hurdle - not the money but your mind. Get everyone in the car and start driving around looking at houses. Go count the stars!

Friend, you serve a big God! You serve a great God! You serve a faithful God! God is not limited by your minimum wage job. He is not limited by your lack of education. He is not limited by the country you are in. You could be a farmer in the bush of Kenya and have a big beautiful house. You could be a waiter at a restaurant making minimum wage and tips and have a beautiful house. Stop looking at all those things. God isn't looking at those things and if He isn't looking at those things, neither should you.

As long as we are considering the circumstances, what we are truly saying is, "God isn't big enough." Like I talked about with your vision board, you need to get a picture of a house you desire and slap copies of it everywhere in your house - put it on your bathroom mirror, on your refrigerator, inside the kitchen cabinets and on the dash of your vehicle. Do like Abraham and count the stars! Look at it enough until you stop "wowing" and start believing. *Circumstances do not move God, but God can't move for you if circumstances are moving you.*

CHAPTER 11
START DECLARING WHAT IS YOURS

2 Corinthians 4:13 NKJV
And since we have the same spirit of faith, according to what is written, "I believed and therefore I spoke," we also believe and therefore speak.

Faith speaks! I believe and therefore I speak. What are you speaking about your house and its furnishings? Friend, you can have what you say. Our world we live in was created by God's words and the world we personally experience is created by our words. You need to get these scriptures I gave you in the first section and start declaring them over your life! Your declarations are one easy way you can begin renewing your mind and making what seems big become small. If you grew up in poverty, you must get rid of that poverty mindset. You need to change your stinking thinking!

BELIEVING GOD FOR A HOUSE

Do you call yourself a renter or a home owner? Do you call your house blessed and filled with precious things or do you call your house cursed and filled with junk? You might need to change what you call yourself and your situation! It is interesting to me that when God started working on Abraham's faith, *not only did He work on Abraham's vision, God also worked on Abraham's mouth.*

Genesis 17:5 NLT
What's more, I am changing your name. It will no longer be Abram. Instead, you will be called Abraham, for you will be the father of many nations.

Abraham's original name was Abram. The name *Abram* meant *father* but was more along the definition of a social father rather than a biological one. Now we know that before God changed his name, Abram was a very rich man and had hundreds of people in his oversight; however, he and his wife did not have a child. So God changed Abram's name to Abraham which meant *father of many nations;* now everywhere Abraham went, he was declaring, "Hi, I'm the father of many nations" even though he and Sarah didn't have a child. Over time, with Abraham's vision changing and his confession changing, his believing changed.

Your words are important! Your words will cause things to come into existence. Your words will enable you to go past what the world says is impossible. Your words will allow you to go past your education, salary, race and location. Start opening your mouth and declaring some things! Faith is the substance of things, but faith can't be released without you opening your mouth.

Your words not only are the releasers of your faith, but they are also the locators of your faith. Anyone can make positive confessions when things are good; however, it is the words coming out of your mouth when times are tough that I am interested in. When you are under pressure, that is when your true beliefs are manifested through your words.

When you are under pressure, this is where you need to watch what you say. We all go through times when it seems all Hell is breaking loose against us - but this is where you do not waver in your confession. I don't care if it looks absolutely impossible and everyone around you is telling you it's impossible - don't you change your confession.

Hebrews 10:23 NKJV
Let us hold fast the confession of our hope without wavering, for He who promised is faithful.

Hold fast to the promises of God and let them keep coming out of your mouth. You will have what you say! Jesus said that; not me. Jesus said if you believe in your heart and confess it with your mouth, you will have it. It is the way you receive salvation and it is the way you receive all the promises of God - including your house and everything in it!

CHAPTER 12
BE LED BY THE HOLY SPIRIT

Romans 8:14 AMP
For all who are allowing themselves to be led by the Spirit of God are sons of God.

I have found that there is so much more to God's system of financial increase than just having a positive confession and throwing some money in the offering bucket. We must also be led by the Holy Spirit. The Holy Spirit knows where your future house is located and He also knows how to get that house to you.

There has to be action to our faith. You can't just sit on your couch all day making positive confessions and waiting for someone to knock on your door with the keys to your new house. There must be action to your faith and this is where you must listen and be led by the Holy Spirit.

You may find Him lead you to drive to a particular

neighborhood and that's where you discover your house. He may lead you into a new business opportunity through which your house comes through. The Holy Spirit may lead you to move to another state, take another job and through those moves, He provides the avenue for the house. Isaiah 1:19 says, "If you are willing and obedient, you will eat the good of the land." *Obedience to what He is telling you to do is key to the good things God has in store for you.*

The greatest financial miracles Lacy and I have seen in our lives have come in the form of being led by the Holy Spirit, sowing financial seed and God blessing us with real estate. Our first venture into this was in our second year of marriage. I was working on my master's degree in counseling at Lamar University and I went the same route to school each night; however, one particular night, I had this slight prompting to go a different way.

I was driving down Highland Avenue in Beaumont, Texas and took a right into this small housing addition. As I turned into the neighborhood, there was a realtor putting his real estate sign out front. For some reason, I had a tremendous pull in my spirit that I needed to get this house. Now understand: Lacy and I were broke and I had a massive amount of debt from college, but I didn't let those things become factors. I got out of my car and approached the realtor about the house.

It was a small two bedroom house that had just been

foreclosed on by the bank. All the bank wanted was what was owed: $10,900. Well, I didn't have $11,000 but I knew I could get a debt consolidation loan for all my debt! So I called the bank that day and was able to get a loan for $12,000 and bought the house.

Now you have to understand this: I had never done repairs on a house, much less flipped a house for a profit. I had no tools and no skills, but I had $1100 to buy some tools and make some repairs. This was a major step of faith for us, but we took the leap!

With some new flooring, new paint and touching up a few minor things, we rented it out for six months at $450 per month. After six months, we sold that little house for $18,000 to another investor. By listening to the Holy Spirit and disregarding my current circumstances, Lacy and I made a little over $5,000. At that point in our lives, that was huge; it was more than two months of my current salary! Not only was I thankful for the money, but I was thankful that God was showing us step by step how we could prosper despite our circumstances.

The first house we bought in Arkansas came the same way. Because of the financial disaster we had been in due to leaving Texas, we had been renting a house for two years. In order to take the church in Arkansas, it required us to leave within a few weeks and for us to walk away from our business. As a result, we were in a financial mess. Since we knew we couldn't get a home loan for a few more years, we decided to find a cheaper rent house and start saving our money to buy land and build as the money came in.

So we set out looking for a cheaper place to rent and during our search, we came across a house that fit our needs. It was decent size, had a fenced back yard and fit our monthly budget. Yet I remember after the owner showed us the house and asked if we wanted it, I had a check in my spirit about it.

I remember sitting in the car talking about it with Lacy; we both agreed it wasn't the right house - even though the size, location and price was what we were looking for. We would have been saving $300 a month and desperately needed it, but we passed on that particular rent house.

Two weeks later, Lacy found an add online for a house for rent that was on ten acres and was the same rent as the one we looked at two weeks prior. Little did we know this house was being foreclosed on. We got in touch with the owner and worked out a deal to do an owner finance for the amount she owed to the bank.

After living there for five years, we sold that property and made a profit of over $120,000! But think about this: we could have missed out on that phenomenal blessing of God if we would have chosen to disregard the leading of the Holy Spirit on the rent house we turned down. Think about that! *If we would* *have been led by money instead of the Holy Spirit, we would have missed out on $120,000 just so we could be in a rent house saving $300 per month.*

If we would have disobeyed, we very well could have been in that cheaper rent house today, asking God, "When are you going to give us our house? We have been standing, believing, sowing, confessing and we are still waiting! What's the deal?"

There are so many people that have missed out on their God deal of a house because they chose to not be led by the Holy Spirit and instead chose to be led by their circumstances. Friend, it pays to be led by the Holy Spirit!

CHAPTER 13
INCREASE YOUR GIVING

Philippians 4:19 AMP
And my God will liberally supply (fill until full) your every need according to His riches in glory in Christ Jesus.

We have seen that it is God's will for you to have a house. We have seen that it is a need and God has promised to meet it, but no matter how you try to spin it, it will still require money for you to buy your house. It will also take more than you just sitting on the couch and quoting, "My God shall supply all my needs!" It's important to keep in context the statement Paul made to the Philippians. This verse is quoted all the time by people believing for things, but it's never kept in the context of what Paul was actually telling them.

Philippians 4:15-19 AMP
15 And you Philippians know that in the early days of preaching the gospel, after I left Macedonia, no church shared with me in the matter of giving and receiving except you alone; 16 for even in Thessalonica you sent a gift more than once for my needs. 17 Not that I seek the

> gift itself, but I do seek the profit which increases to your [heavenly] account [the blessing which is accumulating for you]. 18 But I have received everything in full and more; I am amply supplied, having received from Epaphroditus the gifts you sent me. They are the fragrant aroma of an offering, an acceptable sacrifice which God welcomes and in which He delights. 19 And my God will liberally supply (fill until full) your every need according to His riches in glory in Christ Jesus.

Notice the reason Paul said, "My God shall supply all your needs" was in relation to the Phillipian church giving. Paul said, "Because you gave to support this ministry, God will liberally supply your every need." I like the Message Translation of verse 17.

> **Philippians 4:17 MSG**
> Even while I was in Thessalonica, you helped out—and not only once, but twice. Not that I'm looking for handouts, but I do want you to experience the blessing that issues from generosity.

Paul said, "I want you to experience the blessing that issues from generosity!" This was a spiritual truth regarding giving. He wasn't talking about a spiritual ribbon you get for doing something nice; Paul is talking about a financial blessing: money.

The number one hindrance to people buying their first house, furnishing their house or upgrading to a bigger house is money. It doesn't take a doctoral degree to figure out you need money to buy a house! So the question is, "How do I get more money for my house?" Well, let me show you the short version of what

Increase Your Giving

God has to say about financial increase.

All throughout the Bible, when it comes to financial increase, God never mentions you getting a second or third job. Now I'm not downplaying work in any way. Anyone that knows me knows that I am a firm believer in working hard. I understand there are times when you do what you need to do in order to support yourself and your family; however, what good are you to your family if they only see you between shifts? What good are you to your spouse if you are always tired and cranky because you are constantly working? That isn't God's plan for you.

Yes, we are to work; however, our job was never meant to be our source of finances. Our job is a major channel for finances to flow, but it was never intended to be our source of finances. God is our source - not our job. There are many channels, but only one Source.

When it comes to finances, giving has always been God's way of financial increase. I know it seems counterintuitive, but if you need money, you need to give more. If you need a house, you need to increase your giving.

Proverbs 11:24-25 NLT
24 Give freely and become more wealthy; be stingy and lose everything. 25 The generous will prosper;those who refresh others will themselves be refreshed.

BELIEVING GOD FOR A HOUSE

Poverty Isn't Due To A Lack Of Money

Poverty isn't due to a lack of money; poverty is due to holding onto money that you should have given. Notice this powerful truth: when you increase your giving, you increase your living; when you decrease your giving, you decrease your living. God didn't say get a third job and become more wealthy; He said give more!

Friend, growing up, I thought education and hard work would cause me to prosper. I worked extremely hard - sometimes working two and three jobs. I worked hard in school and obtained my bachelor's degree, my master's degree, a teaching certification and my doctoral degree. Yes, those things will bring certain benefits and open some doors, but I never seemed to get ahead. With all of that, I was still in debt and physically and emotionally exhausted. I was looking to all those things as my source!

It wasn't until I began to discover the truths of God's Word concerning giving that things began to change for Lacy and I. We began to tap into God's law of financial increase and slowly things began to change. It didn't happen overnight, but as Lacy and I began to increase our giving, we saw our living begin to increase.

2 Corinthians 9:6-11 NKJV
6 But this I say: He who sows sparingly will also reap sparingly, and he who sows bountifully will also reap

bountifully. 7 So let each one give as he purposes in his heart, not grudgingly or of necessity; for God loves a cheerful giver. 8 And God is able to make all grace abound toward you, that you, always having all sufficiency in all things, may have an abundance for every good work. 9 As it is written: "He has dispersed abroad, He has given to the poor; His righteousness endures forever."10 Now may He who supplies seed to the sower, and bread for food, supply and multiply the seed you have sown and increase the fruits of your righteousness, 11 while you are enriched in everything for all liberality, which causes thanksgiving through us to God.

God's system of financial increase is sowing and reaping. I know some people don't agree with that but it's just Bible. It is a spiritual law that you can not change just as much as you can not change the law of gravity. When I start talking to God about needing something, almost every time He starts talking to me about giving something. From that seed sown, it results in money coming my way. Now, I'm not saying the result every time is someone just walking up and handing you cash. The harvest on that seed sown may end up being an open door for a new business opportunity or wisdom on where to go and what to do. It will require you to still do something, but the end result will be the thing you for which you were believing.

Sowing Seed Is Never Convenient

I've also found that when He starts talking to me about giving something, it has never been convenient either! Why? Because you need that money! In reality though, you need to give that money so God can send more money back to you. Notice what God said in 2 Corinthians 9:7-8.

> **2 Corinthians 9:7-8 NKJV**
> **7 So let each one give as he purposes in his heart, not grudgingly or of necessity; for God loves a cheerful giver.**
> **8 And God is able to make all grace abound toward you, that you, always having all sufficiency in all things.**

Notice the connection between giving and increase. "So let each one give...and God is able to make all grace abound toward you so that you have all sufficiency in all things." Verse 8 sounds a whole lot like Philippians 4:19 doesn't it?

> **Philippians 4:19 AMP**
> **And my God will liberally supply (fill until full) your every need according to His riches in glory in Christ Jesus.**

But remember the context of this statement? God "liberally supplying every need" was in relation to giving. In 2 Corinthians 9:7-8, God making "all grace abound so that you have all sufficiency in all things" was in relation to giving.

You can't quote "My God shall supply all my needs" if you aren't a giver. Do you know why? Because you don't qualify. You can't quote "God is making all grace abound towards me and I have all sufficiency in all things" if you aren't a giver. Why? Because to qualify, you must be a giver. The good news is we all have the ability to give!

Increase Your Giving

So you want a house but you are low on funds? Increase your giving! If you need money, you need to start giving. Now I am not talking about just giving all your money away and this certainly isn't some get rich quick scheme. This is where you need to learn to be led by the Holy Spirit in your giving.

Every time Lacy and I have had a financial need, we have sowed a financial seed. When I would go to God about the situation, He would end up having us to sow financially to a person or to a ministry.

We have story after story of how God blessed us financially because of the financial seed we sowed. It didn't happen because we walked up to the first homeless person we could find and gave them some cash; it happened because we both sensed the Holy Spirit leading us to give a specific amount to a specific person and then walked through the doors He opened.

There have been times God led us to give to a particular ministry and times we gave to a particular individual. Sometimes the ministry or person He led us to give to - it didn't seem like in the natural they really needed the money, but that isn't the reason we give. Don't be led by circumstances in your giving; be led by the Holy Spirit!

Giving Gave Us Real Estate

When we had started our first church in Texas, after the first

BELIEVING GOD FOR A HOUSE

nine months, we had outgrown the little 4,000 sq ft building we were leasing. I wanted our own building and began talking to God about it. He told us as a church to sow $10,000 to Rhema Bible Training Center; the only problem was our church only had $500 in our bank account! The following Sunday, I told our church what God was leading us to do and we had $4500 come in the offering. At that time, it was one of the largest offerings we had ever had - but we still only had $5,000.

Well, two days later, I got a check in the mail from a church three hours away. Do you know how much the check was for? They sent us a check for $5000 and they had no idea what we were believing for nor what God had told me. Isn't that amazing? God told us to sow a seed we didn't have, but we trusted God and *He gave us the seed - not to eat but to sow!*

Well, we sowed that $10,000 and do you know what happened? Through a series of various events, the city gave us $100,000 and we bought a 1.2 million dollar building for $550,000 with no money down.

Friend, how is it possible for a small start up church with $500 in the bank to buy a one million dollar building six months later and have $100,000 in the bank? It wasn't because I was smart; it was because we were led by the Holy Spirit and gave what and where He told us to give and walked through the doors He opened.

Don't ever forget 2 Corinthians 9:10-11. If you don't have the seed, He will give you the seed! I am living proof!

2 Corinthians 9:10-11 NKJV
10 Now may He who supplies seed to the sower, and bread for food, supply and multiply the seed you have sown and increase the fruits of your righteousness, 11 while you are enriched.

Not only will God give you the seed, He will multiply that seed you have sown and bring increase your way so that you are enriched. Notice the four letters in the middle of enriched? RICH! How do you increase? How do you become wealthy? Being led by the Holy Spirit in your sowing and reaping.

So remember in the last chapter, I told you about our first house in Arkansas? Well, there is more to the story I want to share with you.

We were not in a position to buy a house and had a massive amount of debt on us but we were believing God. We had decided to lower our monthly budget by finding a cheaper rent house and believing God for some land on which to build. He led us to sow $1000 for our land, which was all we had in our savings account, to our friends Ken and Trudi Blount.

Well, two weeks later, we came across the house that was being foreclosed on. We thought we were just looking for a rent house; we had no clue it was the land we were beliving for!

We worked out a deal to catch the individual up on the mortgage and do an owner finance for what they owed to the bank. The house appraised for $245,000 at the time and we bought it for $150,000. Four years later, we sold that same property for almost $300,000!

How does someone go from having $1000 in the bank and jacked up credit to making a profit of over $120,000? Sowing seed! We listened to the Holy Spirit, sowed the money to the Blounts, passed up the rent house that would have saved us $300 a month and then went to look at a house for rent that no one knew was being foreclosed on!

Friend, I have so many stories of financial increase from sowing and reaping. Our latest house came from sowing seed and being obedient to the leading of the Holy Spirit and it was the greatest God deal yet. The build value on this property was 1.5 million that we got for less than half of its value and it came filled with some beautiful things. It has six bedrooms, eight bathrooms, four fireplaces, a swimming pool, tennis court and lots of other things that were thrown in for free. I've been wanting a baby grand piano for years and do you know what? The house came with one! In addition to all the extras, the property has the potential of generating additional income for us!

I used to get nervous when God told us to give; now I get excited. *Every time God tells us to give, I know He is not only trying to get something to someone else, He is also trying to get something to me.*

Don't allow your bank account to tell you what you can have and can't have. *If you have seed, you can increase.* You may not have the education or finances others may have, but you always have seed and you always have the Holy Spirit. When you operate according to God's system of increase, the circumstances of life can not hold you back.

One word from God will change your life my friend. Do what God tells you to do. His wisdom will blow open hidden doors for you. Go where He tells you to go and give where He tells you to give and watch that seed multiply into a massive harvest. Just like when you plant a seed in the ground, you don't see a fruit bearing plant pop out the very next day. I can't guarantee you when the harvest will show up, but I can guarantee that when you are obedient to the leading of the Holy Spirit, you will have a harvest.

If you will make giving a lifestyle, you will see your lifestyle change for the better! Your job is to be the sower; God's job is to be the multiplier. You do your job, let God do His job and you will not only have your house, but you will also be in a position to be a major blessing to your world.

CHAPTER 14
START PRAISING GOD

Romans 4:19-21 NKJV
19 And not being weak in faith, he did not consider his own body, already dead (since he was about a hundred years old), and the deadness of Sarah's womb. 20 He did not waver at the promise of God through unbelief, but was strengthened in faith, giving glory to God, 21 and being fully convinced that what He had promised He was also able to perform.

There will be times during this process of believing the Word for your house and getting the keys to your house in which opportunities will come for you to get frustrated. There will be times of wondering "What is taking so long?" in which there will be perfect opportunities to waver in your belief - but it is in these times that instead of complaining, you need to start praising.

What would you do if someone gave you the keys to your house today? You would start shouting! You might even do a dance and run all over the room! Well, what are you waiting for? Why would you thank God for your house only when you physically are in it? Remember Hebrews 11:1?

> **Hebrews 11:1 AMP**
> **Now faith is the assurance (title deed, confirmation) of things hoped for (divinely guaranteed), and the evidence of things not seen [the conviction of their reality—faith comprehends as fact what cannot be experienced by the physical senses].**

Faith is the title deed. When you believed it and received it in your spirit and soul, that's when you got it - so that is when you should start praising God! Romans 15:13 says, "May the God of hope fill you with all peace and joy in believing." Why would you be at peace and full of joy while in faith? Because you know you have it! If you know you have it, you can start thanking God for it!

This is how we know Abraham got to the point that he chose not to waiver in his faith. Instead of taking the opportunities to get weak and into unbelief, he chose to praise God! While Abraham was praising God, despite impossible circumstances, he was growing strong in faith.

Friend, sometimes, you just need a praise break. If you can have a smoke break, a drink break, a restroom break, etc., you can have a praise break too! If you are getting down, that's your sign you have allowed yourself to get your eyes on the circumstances and off of the promises. It is your sign you need to start giving some glory to God for what He has done and what

He is about to do! You don't need to be in church and have the Hammond B3 screaming in the background. You don't need your special handkerchief and you don't need to be in front of people. Sometimes you just need to get off by yourself and have a praise break.

I remember one time I got to that point. Lacy and I had been living in Arkansas about six months and because of our decision to leave Texas and take on a ministry work in Arkansas, we were in a major financial disaster. Because of having to leave Texas so quickly, we had to walk away from our business. In leaving, we found out our director had been embezzling money and didn't pay taxes. It left us with over $75,000 in business debt, our house foreclosed on and creditors calling our phones and knocking on our doors - I was at an absolute low. But I remember one night, I had enough of feeling sorry for myself. I went outside away from where anyone could see or hear me and I started shouting and praising God.

I had no idea of how He would get us out of this mess. It was a massive step of faith because it didn't look like the wise thing to do in the natural. I knew He sent us and as a result, He was responsible for taking care of us. I kept holding onto what Jesus said regarding leaving things for the sake of the Gospel.

> **Mark 10:29-30**
> **29 So Jesus answered and said, "Assuredly, I say to you, there is no one who has left house or brothers or sisters or father or mother [a]or wife or children or [b]lands, for My sake and the gospel's, 30 who shall not receive**

a hundredfold now in this time—houses and brothers and sisters and mothers and children and lands, with persecutions—and in the age to come, eternal life.

We were obedient in following His leading and so I was praising Him in advance for what He was already doing behind the scenes and what He was about to do.

Little did I know that what Satan had been doing to try and stop us - it was all a set up and God was about to prosper us like we had never experienced before!

Don't Be Moved By A Clock

Friend, don't fall into the trap of feeling sorry for yourself and thinking after a period of time that it isn't going to happen. God isn't moved by a clock and neither should you. Don't look at the calendar. Don't look at the clock. Don't look at the situation. Don't look at your dire circumstances. Just keep your eyes on the promises of God! You need to realize that anytime money is involved, people will be involved - and sometimes people are slow to obey and slow to move.

It's different in the area of finances than it is in the area of healing. You experiencing God's promise of healing doesn't require the involvement of other people; it is just you and Him. When it comes to experiencing God's promises in the area of finances, it requires the involvement of other people. It requires God speaking to people, those people hearing and then obeying.

If they refuse to obey, God has to move on to someone else and the cycle continues until He finds a willing person.

Money doesn't fall out of the sky; it comes through people. Houses don't just appear out of thin air; they require people. When you have been sowing and confessing, don't grow weary in doing good. Don't let time get you into unbelief. Get your eyes off the clock and keep your eyes on Him. God doesn't always pay on Fridays, but He always pays up!

Don't Fall Into The Comparison Trap

You will find there will also be times to get offended when you see other people prospering and getting their house. Sometimes it is easy to get into a comparison trap; I've seen that happen with many people including myself. Instead of getting offended when someone got their house before you - rejoice with them and then declare, "I'm next!"

I remember when God blessed us with our first house in Arkansas; it was what I called a "God deal." Lacy and I were so excited about it. We had been through so much but had been faithful in our sowing and obedience to God's leading and it had certainly paid off.

This one particular Sunday, this lady had heard about the blessing that had happened for us. I'll never forget her response. She said to us, "Well, that's not fair. I've been believing God for over ten years for a house with lots of land." Friend, the gift of slap started to come on me, but I withheld. It made me angry because she had no idea what we had given up and everything we had done to be at that point. Instead of rejoicing with us, she was offended at us! You will have a hard time receiving something from God when you're offended at someone else.

Get Your Praise On

Don't be like that woman. When your friends and fellow Christian brothers and sisters prosper, rejoice with them. Thank God for what He did for them and thank God for what He's doing for you.

Friend, start praising and thanking God right now! You might just need to shout about it. You might need to dance a jig. Get off of your couch and stop feeling sorry for yourself. Lay out the promises of God and let the devil know that despite all he's tried to do, it will come to no avail. Let all of Hell know that you believe God! Let all of Heaven know that you believe God!

Begin to declare the end from the beginning...that you will not end up where you started. The latter of your life will be greater than the former. Friend, faith in God is the great equalizer and the excuse eliminator. God's promises are Yes and Amen; not maybe and we hope so. Get your praise on because your house is on the way!

HOUSE SCRIPTURES

Deuteronomy 6:10-11 AMP When the Lord your God brings you into the land which He swore to your fathers, to Abraham, Isaac, and Jacob, to give you, with great and goodly cities which you did not build, and houses full of all good things which you did not fill, and cisterns hewn out which you did not hew, and vineyards and olive trees which you did not plant.

Deuteronomy 8:11-14 NKJV 11 "Beware that you do not forget the Lord your God by not keeping His commandments, His judgments, and His statutes which I command you today, 12 lest—when you have eaten and are full, and have built beautiful houses and dwell in them; 13 and when your herds and your flocks multiply, and your silver and your gold are multiplied, and all that you have is multiplied; 14 when your heart is lifted up, and you forget the Lord your God.

Deuteronomy 8:18 AMP But you shall remember [with profound respect] the Lord your God, for it is He who is giving you power to make wealth, that He may confirm His covenant which He swore (solemnly promised) to your fathers, as it is this day.

Psalm 16:5-6 MSG My choice is you, God, first and only. And now I find I'm your choice! You set me up with a house and yard. And then you made me your heir!

Psalm 18:19 AMP He brought me forth also into a large place; He was delivering me because He was pleased with me and delighted in me.

Psalm 66:12 KJV Thou hast caused men to ride over our heads; we went through fire and through water: but thou broughtest us out into a wealthy place.

Psalm 68:6 AMP God places the solitary in families and gives the desolate a home in which to dwell; He leads the prisoners out to prosperity; but the rebellious dwell in a parched land.

Psalm 107:7 AMP He led them forth by the straight and right way, that they might go to a city where they could establish their homes.

Psalm 112:3 MSG Their houses brim with wealth and a generosity that never runs dry.

Psalm 122:7 AMP May peace be within your walls and prosperity within your palaces!

Proverbs 3:33 NIV The Lord's curse is on the house of the wicked, but he blesses the home of the righteous.

Proverbs 12:7 AMP The wicked are overthrown and are not, but the house of the [uncompromisingly] righteous shall stand.

Proverbs 14:11 NLT The house of the wicked will be destroyed, but the tent of the godly will flourish.

Proverbs 15:6 AMP In the house of the [uncompromisingly] righteous is great [priceless] treasure.

Proverbs 24:3-4 AMP Through skillful and godly Wisdom is a house (a life, a home, a family) built, and by understanding it is established [on a sound and good foundation], and by knowledge shall its chambers [of every area] be filled with all precious and pleasant riches.

Proverbs 24:4 NIV Through knowledge its rooms are filled with rare and beautiful treasures.

Proverbs 24:27 AMP [Put first things first.] Prepare your work outside and get it ready for yourself in the field; and afterward build your house and establish a home.

Isaiah 32:18 MSG My people will live in a peaceful neighborhood—in safe houses, in quiet gardens.

Isaiah 65:21 NIV They will build houses and dwell in them; they will plant vineyards and eat their fruit.

Isaiah 65:22 MSG No more building a house that some outsider takes over. No more planting fields that some enemy confiscates.

Jeremiah 29:5 AMP Build yourselves houses and dwell in them; plant gardens and eat the fruit of them.

John 14:2 NKJV In my Father's house are many mansions: if it were not so, I would have told you. I go to prepare a place for you.

2 Corinthians 9:7-8 NKJV So let each one give as he purposes in his heart, not grudgingly or of necessity; for God loves a cheerful giver. And God is able to make all grace abound toward you, that you, always having all sufficiency in all things, may have an abundance for every good work.

ABOUT THE AUTHOR

Chad and Lacy Gonzales are graduates of Rhema Bible Training College. Chad holds a M.Ed. in Counseling from Lamar University and a D.Min. from School of Bible Theology and Seminary University.

With an emphasis on one's union with Christ, Chad brings a powerful and practical message of faith and grace to the world. The mission of Chad Gonzales Ministries is to connect people to God so they can manifest God to their world. Declaring the Gospel with simplicity, boldness and a touch of humor, mighty miracles of healing are common in their meetings.

Together with their son Jake, they minister around the world teaching and proving that Jesus loves, Jesus heals and Jesus wants to work through you!

OTHER BOOKS AVAILABLE

Aliens
An Alternate Reality
Eight Percent
Fearless
God's Will Is You Healed
Healed
Making Right Decisions
Naturally Supernatural
Possessors Of Life
Think Like Jesus
Walking In The Miraculous
What's Next

The Supernatural Life Podcast

Check out The Supernatural Life Podcast with Chad Gonzales! New episodes are available each month designed to help you connect with God on a deeper level and live the supernatural life God desires for you to have!

The Healing Academy is an outreach of Chad Gonzales Ministries to help the everyday believer learn to walk according to the standard of Jesus in the ministry of healing.

Jesus said in John 14:12 that whoever believes in Him would do the same works and even greater works. Through *The Healing Academy,* it is our goal to raise the standard of the healing ministry in the Church and manifest the ministry of Jesus in the marketplace.

The Healing Academy is available by video training series as well as in person training. For more information, please visit www.ChadGonzales.com/healing

SALVATION AND THE BAPTISM OF THE HOLY SPIRIT

Dear friend, it is the desire of God that everyone accepts His free gift of salvation. God sent the greatest gift Heaven had so the world could be set free; that precious gift was Jesus! Despite knowing the mistakes you would make, He died for you anyway. Jesus knew the mistakes you would make, yet He still climbed up on the cross. Why? His love was greater than your sin.

Romans 10:9-10 says if you will confess Jesus as your Lord and Savior and believe that He arose from the dead, you will be saved. You see, salvation has nothing to do with works. It doesn't matter what church you belong to, how many little old ladies you help across the street or how much you give the church. You cannot earn salvation; you cannot buy salvation; you must simply accept salvation.

Another free gift that God has provided is the Baptism of the Holy Spirit. In Acts 2, we find the Baptism of the Holy Spirit being given to the Church. God desires that you be filled with His Spirit with the evidence of speaking in tongues.

God said in Acts 2:38 that this life changing gift was for everyone, not just a select few. It wasn't just for those living in Bible days; it was given to everyone who would accept Jesus as

Lord and Savior. Jesus said the purpose of the Baptism of the Holy Spirit was so you could be a witness with power! You'll find that when you receive the Baptism of the Holy Spirit, it allows you to operate in the fullness of God's power and be a blessing to the entire world. Essentially, you could say that salvation gets you into a relationship with God and the Baptism of the Holy Spirit helps you get others into a relationship with God.

Regardless of who you are, God has a plan for your life. He wants you to be successful, have all your needs met and live a life of victory. God wants every day of your life to be a day full of peace and joy, but it all begins with Jesus being your Lord and Savior. If you have never accepted Jesus as your Lord and Savior, please pray this prayer with me right now:

Jesus, I confess that I am a sinner. I realize I can't do this on my own. I believe with my heart and confess with my mouth that you died on the cross for my sins and sicknesses and arose from the dead. I ask you to be the Lord and Savior of my life. I thank you for forgiving me of my sins and loving me enough to give your life for me. I thank you that I am now a child of God! I now ask you for the Baptism of the Holy Spirit. You said in Your Word that it was a free gift so I receive it now. I thank you for my Heavenly prayer language!

We encourage you to become involved in a solid Bible based church. If you need help finding a church in your area, we would be more than happy to help.

Begin reading your Bible and praying in the Spirit daily. Now it is time to start developing your relationship with your Heavenly Father and growing in the Lord - and don't forget to tell someone about what Jesus did for you! Remember that God is good and He has good things in store for you!

If you prayed this prayer, would like assistance in locating a local church or this book has impacted your life, we would love to hear from you!

www.ChadGonzales.com

Printed in Great Britain
by Amazon